J. C. BUSH SCHOOL

Eye on the Universe

The Life of an Astronaut

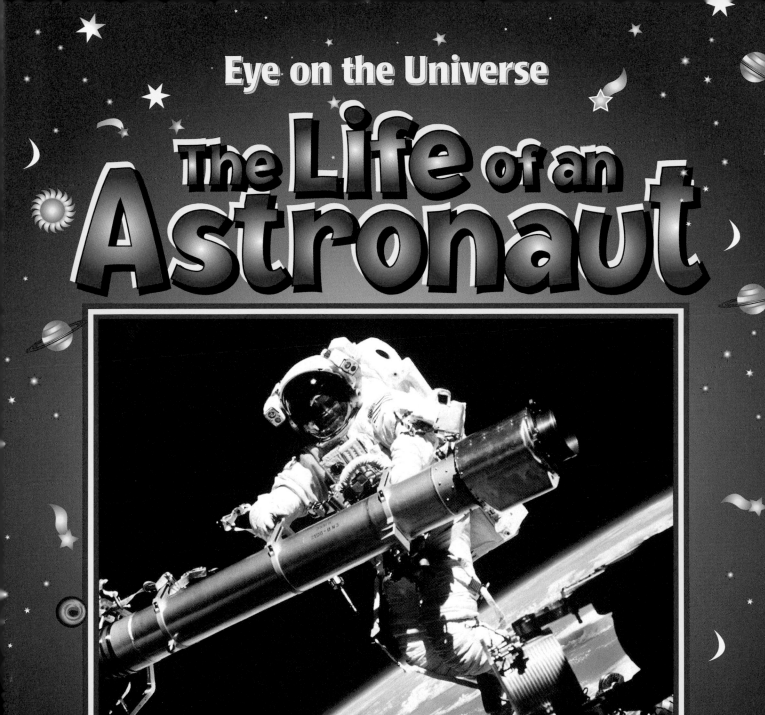

Niki Walker
Crabtree Publishing Company

www.crabtreebooks.com

Eye on the Universe

Created by Bobbie Kalman

To Nolan

Editor-in-Chief
Bobbie Kalman

Author
Niki Walker

Managing editor
Lynda Hale

Project editor
John Crossingham

Editors
Kate Calder
Hannelore Sotzek
Heather Levigne

Computer design
Lynda Hale

Production coordinator
Hannelore Sotzek

Photo researcher
Jaimie Nathan

Special thanks to
NASA; Mary Thompson and U.S. Space & Rocket Center; U.S. SPACE CAMP®

Consultant
Edd Davis, Media Relations Director,
U.S. Space & Rocket Center, U.S. SPACE CAMP® and Aviation Challenge

Photographs
NASA: front cover, pages 1, 8, 9 (bottom), 10, 11, 13 (both), 15, 16, 17,
    19 (both), 21 (bottom), 22, 23, 24 (both), 25 (top)
U.S. SPACE CAMP®: pages 30, 31 (both)
Other photographs by Digital Stock and Eyewire, Inc.

Illustrations
Bonna Rouse

Digital prepress
Embassy Graphics

Printer
Worzalla Publishing Company

Crabtree Publishing Company

www.crabtreebooks.com   1-800-387-7650

PMB 16A
350 Fifth Avenue,
Suite 3308
New York, NY
10118

612 Welland Avenue
St. Catharines,
Ontario
Canada
L2M 5V6

73 Lime Walk
Headington,
Oxford
OX3 7AD
United Kingdom

Cataloging-in-Publication Data
Walker, Niki
    The life of an astronaut

p. cm. — (Eye on the universe)
Includes index.

ISBN 0-86505-683-8 (library bound) — ISBN 0-86505-693-5 (pbk.)
This book describes the requirements, training, tasks, and duties
of astronauts and covers such topics as operating a spacecraft and
living in space.

1. Astronautics—Juvenile literature. 2. Astronauts—Juvenile
literature. 3. Space flight—Juvenile literature. [1. Astronauts.
2. Occupations. 3. Astronautics. 4. Space flight.] I. Title. II. Series:
Kalman, Bobbie. Eye on the universe.

TL793 .W323 2001   j629.45—dc21   LC 00-060387
                                                                                          CIP

Contents

What are astronauts?

Astronauts perform one of the most exciting jobs imaginable! They are well-trained men and women who fly into space. Astronauts are often compared to explorers who sailed in search of new places. In fact, the word "astronaut" means "star sailor." Astronauts come from many places including the United States, Russia, Canada, and Europe.

What is a mission?

Each trip astronauts make into space is called a **mission**. The specific goal or task they set out to accomplish on their trip is also called a mission. Sometimes the mission of the astronauts is to explore other planets or the Moon. On each mission, astronauts also record information about living and working in space. On some missions, the astronauts may release, repair, or retrieve **satellites**, perform experiments, or help construct the **International Space Station**, or **ISS** (see pages 7 and 21).

Space suit protection

Traveling into space may be exciting, but it is also very dangerous. In space, there is no air to breathe. Without air, there is no air pressure. Without air pressure, human lungs collapse and blood feels as though it is boiling. The temperatures drop to -250° F (-157°C) in darkness and soar to 250°F (121°C) in sunlight. Humans cannot survive in space without the protection of a space suit.

Spacecraft and space suits, such as the one worn by the astronaut in this photo, allow astronauts to maintain a safe body temperature and air pressure level.

Astronaut history

The first "astronaut" was not a person. It was a dog named Laika! She was sent into space in 1951 by the former Soviet Union. Scientists continued to send animals into space to make sure it would be safe for people. In 1961, a Soviet astronaut, or **cosmonaut**, named Yuri Gagarin became the first person in space.

Creating NASA

In 1959, the United States created **NASA**, or the **National Aeronautics and Space Administration**. NASA's first astronauts were seven men from the armed forces. NASA has conducted many **projects**. Each one has included several missions.

From rockets to shuttles

Early spacecraft were much different from those of today. The first spacecraft was a tiny capsule that was used only once. It was launched on the end of a large rocket. Since 1981, NASA crew members have worked aboard larger, reusable spacecraft called **Space Shuttles**. On a Space Shuttle mission, astronauts spend up to thirty days **orbiting**, or circling, Earth.

Exploring space

The first NASA projects were **Mercury**, **Gemini**, and **Apollo**. Each project had certain goals. During project Mercury, the United States' first astronauts went into space. The goal of the Apollo project was to land people on the Moon; on July 20th 1969, astronauts Neil Armstrong and Edwin "Buzz" Aldrin became the first humans to accomplish this goal.

The Apollo 11 rocket as it was on its way to the Moon!

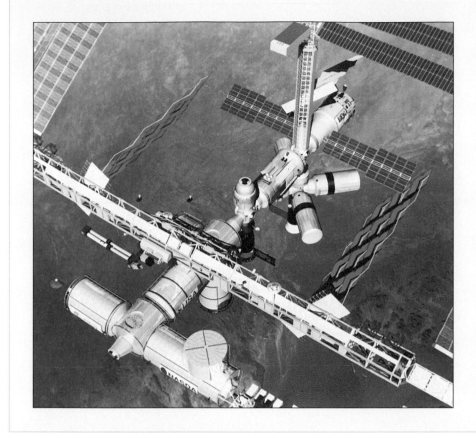

What's next?

In the near future, astronauts will spend long periods of time living aboard the International Space Station. They will conduct experiments and study how space affects their body. NASA is also hoping to use the station as a **launching pad** for missions to the Moon or Mars. For more information on the ISS, see page 21.

Astronaut milestones

April 1961: Yuri Gagarin is the first person in space. He makes the first orbit of Earth.

May 1961: Alan Shepard, Jr. is the first American in space. He does not orbit Earth.

1962: John Glenn, Jr. becomes the first American to orbit Earth.

1963: Cosmonaut Valentina Tereshkova is the first woman in space.

1965: Cosmonaut Aleksey Leonov is the first person to step outside a spacecraft in space.

1966: In project Gemini, astronauts successfully **dock**, or join, two craft in space.

1969: Americans Neil Armstrong and Buzz Aldrin become the first people on the Moon.

1973: The American space station **Skylab** is launched with three astronauts aboard.

1981: The first Space Shuttle, Columbia, is launched.

1983: Sally Ride becomes the first American woman in space.

1986: Russia launches the space station *Mir*.

1994-98: During the Shuttle-*Mir* project, the United States and Russia use Space Shuttles and *Mir* to study life in space further.

The crew

In the past, a spacecraft carried only one or two astronauts who did everything from flying and landing the ship to conducting experiments. In a Space Shuttle, a crew of five to seven astronauts flies on every mission. The crew is made up of two **pilot astronauts** and at least three others who are **mission specialists**. Some missions also include one or two **payload specialists**. Each astronaut in the crew has specific jobs to do.

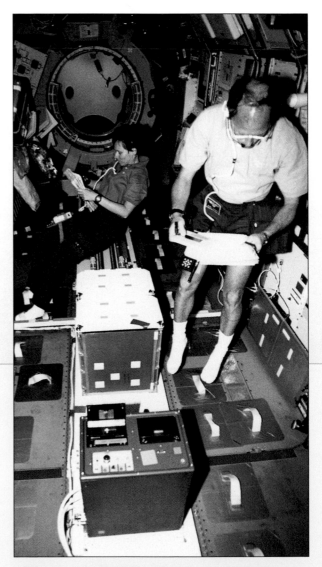

Although payload specialists travel into space, they are not career astronauts. They are experts whose knowledge is needed when dealing with a specific experiment or cargo. These two payload specialists are conducting an experiment during a Shuttle mission.

Who's who in the crew?

One of the pilots acts as the **commander**. The commander is in charge of the mission. He or she is responsible for the safety of the crew and the Shuttle. The other pilot assists the commander. Although they are trained to fly the Shuttle in case of an emergency, it is not their job to do so. The Shuttle is actually controlled by computers on board and on Earth. The commander, however, is responsible for controlling the Shuttle during landing.

Leave everything to me!

Once the Shuttle reaches orbit around Earth, mission specialists carry out most of the work. They perform experiments and keep track of food and water use. They are responsible for the **payload**, or the materials and objects in the shuttle's **cargo bay**. Mission specialists also leave the Shuttle to perform work in space.

Mission specialists use many tools and gadgets to make it easier to work in space. This astronaut even has a checklist attached to her right arm.

Mission Control

Workers at **Mission Control** at the **Johnson Space Center** in Houston, Texas observe the Shuttle and communicate with the astronauts using radios, computers, satellites, and cameras. They also help the crew solve problems and complete tasks. The crew stays in contact with Mission Control almost twenty-four hours a day. The only time they do not communicate with an astronaut is when he or she is asleep. Russia's Mission Control is located in the city of Korolev.

Practice, practice, practice

Every two years, NASA selects about one hundred men and women to be astronaut candidates. Candidates train for one to two years in hope of becoming astronauts. They take classes in **navigation**, **astronomy**, math, **physics**, computers, aircraft safety, and weather. They have a lot to learn before they will even be considered for a position on the Shuttle!

Candidates also train using **simulators**. Simulators are full-sized computerized models of the Shuttle and its controls. There are two Shuttle simulators. The **motion-based simulator**, or **MBS**, shakes and rolls just as the real Shuttle does during its launch and landing. The **fixed-base simulator**, or **FBS**, has all the same controls as the real Shuttle, but it does not move.

*The suspended astronaut is using a device called a **Sky genie** to simulate escaping from a troubled Space Shuttle. To the left is a Shuttle simulator. It has all the buttons and switches found on the real Shuttle.*

Ready for anything

Instructors teach candidates how to work every part of the Shuttle—from the toilet to the oxygen supply. The candidates also practice activities such as meal preparation, housekeeping, and equipment storage. They learn how to respond to hundreds of possible emergencies.

*A **centrifuge** allows astronauts to feel what launch and **reentry**, or returning to Earth, is like. This machine spins at high speeds and creates a force that pushes the astronauts back.*

Astronaut candidates train with parachutes in case they need to make an emergency exit.

Mission training

After about a year of training, NASA selects the men and women who will become full-fledged astronauts. They continue training for at least one year before their first mission. About ten weeks before they launch, the astronauts concentrate on the specific tasks they will perform as part of their mission, such as repairing satellites. The astronauts use computer programs that are created especially to help them train. They also practice working with the leader of their Mission Control team.

Training for weightlessness

One of the most exciting aspects of astronaut training is learning how to work in **microgravity**. Microgravity is another word for weightlessness. In space, everything inside the Shuttle becomes weightless and floats around, including the astronauts! They must learn how to move and perform tasks in this environment.

The "Vomit Comet"

To experience weightlessness, astronauts train in a special jet that flies up and down at very steep angles. As the jet dives, the astronauts become weightless for about twenty seconds. During this time, they practice eating, drinking, and using equipment. The jet is often called the "Vomit Comet" because some people get sick during the flight!

Handle with care

Astronauts use a simulator to learn how to lift objects with the Space Shuttle's robotic arm (see page 18). They practice lifting and setting down helium-filled balloons, which act like weightless cargo.

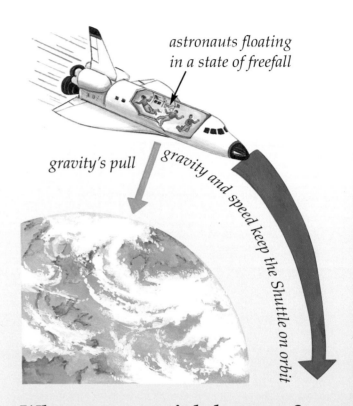

astronauts floating in a state of freefall

gravity's pull

gravity and speed keep the Shuttle on orbit

What causes weightlessness?

Many people think that things in space are weightless because there is no gravity, but this is not true. In fact, Earth's gravity holds the Shuttle **on orbit!** Gravity pulls the Shuttle toward Earth, but the spacecraft moves so quickly that it can travel around the planet without crashing to the ground. The Shuttle and everything inside it are in a state of **free fall**. Free fall also happens when people jump out of planes or ride down the steep hill of a roller coaster.

The inside of the training jet has padded walls and no seats so the candidates can move around safely.

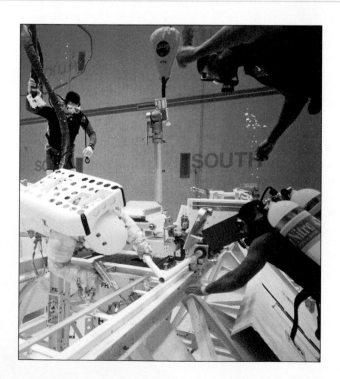

Scuba training

Scuba diving is also used to experience weightlessness. The sensation of being underwater is similar to the feeling of weightlessness in space. Astronauts train in huge water tanks that contain a full-sized model of the Shuttle. They move around the model and perform tasks such as connecting wires and turning screws. Astronauts also wear their space suits along with their scuba gear to get used to moving in them.

Three divers are helping an astronaut train in NASA's giant water tank. The astronaut is using a drill designed for use in space.

Leaving Earth behind

A week before the astronauts launch into space, they are **quarantined**, or isolated from almost everyone, to help prevent them from getting sick. They leave their homes and stay in rooms at the Space Center. When launch day finally arrives, the astronauts are eager to go! They are taken to the launch pad, where the Shuttle awaits. The astronauts climb inside the Shuttle, strap themselves to steel chairs, and wait for the countdown to begin.

visor

helmet

communication equipment

parachute and harness (strapped to back)

gloves

urine collection device, or UCD (inside suit)

long underwear

boots

Launch gear

Astronauts wear a lot of equipment during the launch in case of an emergency exit, or **egress**. During an egress, astronauts leave the Shuttle before it reaches space and parachute back to Earth. The outer layer is the **pressure suit**. If the Shuttle loses air pressure, the suit inflates to keep the astronaut's air pressure steady. Astronauts carry an escape kit that includes a life raft, drinking water, flares, and oxygen bottles.

Liftoff!

NASA is very careful to ensure that the launch runs smoothly. To be sure all is safe, astronauts often must wait inside the Shuttle for two to five hours before the **countdown** starts.

large fuel tank

SRB

3. Just before the Shuttle reaches orbit, the large fuel tank also falls away. The commander uses small **maneuvering rockets** to steer the Shuttle into orbit and then turns off the engines. Gravity keeps the craft moving around Earth—the Shuttle is on orbit.

2. Two minutes after launch, the **solid rocket boosters,** or **SRB**s, fall away. At this point, the Shuttle stops accelerating and gravity's force grows weaker.

1. The Shuttle blasts off with such force that the astronauts feel as though a heavy weight is pushing down on them. It is difficult for them to move or speak.

*These astronauts are testing an **escape basket**. It is used before the launch to exit the Shuttle during an emergency, such as a fuel leak. The baskets slide 200 feet (61 m) from the launching tower to the ground.*

Adjusting to microgravity

Once the Shuttle reaches orbit, all people and objects inside it become weightless. While they are weightless, astronauts notice many changes in their body. Their face gets puffy and their legs become weak. Some astronauts feel as if their nose is stuffed up. Weightlessness feels similar to hanging upside-down on monkey bars.

Growing pains

Astronauts become up to two inches (5 cm) taller in space because the bones in their spinal column spread apart. As their body stretches, their waistline also becomes smaller. Growing so quickly causes most astronauts a great deal of discomfort.

*This astronaut is using a device that measures her **mass** in microgravity.*

Space sickness

Many astronauts suffer from **space sickness**. Being in a weightless environment makes them feel nauseated and causes them to vomit. Before they can work outside the Shuttle in space, all astronauts must wait two days until their body adjusts to microgravity. They cannot risk becoming sick outside the Shuttle.

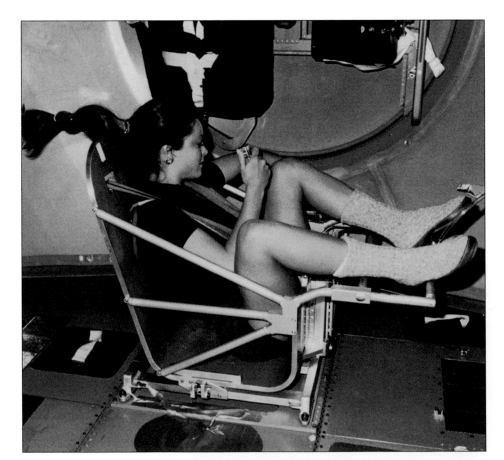

Getting around

Astronauts quickly learn that moving in microgravity takes little effort. A slight push with a finger is enough to send them from one side of the Shuttle to the other! It is important to move slowly around the ship. If astronauts push too hard, they can spin out of control and crash into things.

*Any object that is not secured inside the Shuttle floats around. Astronauts use restraints such as straps, clips, and Velcro® strips to hold themselves and their tools in place. White straps called **footholds** are placed throughout the Shuttle's interior. Astronauts anchor themselves to one spot by slipping their feet into the footholds.*

Astronauts at work

While on orbit, astronauts follow a schedule called a **flight plan**. Mission Control designs the flight plan before the astronauts leave the ground. There is a plan for every day of the mission. Crew members use it to determine when to wake up, exercise, sleep, and perform all the tasks scheduled for the day. Some tasks are performed aboard the Shuttle, whereas others are performed in space.

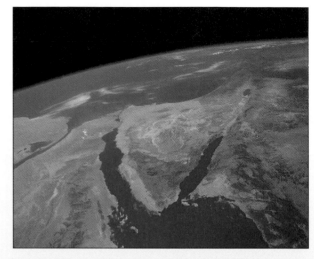

The pictures astronauts take while aboard the Shuttle may help us map Earth.

Deploying payloads

Astronauts use a huge robotic arm to retrieve and **deploy**, or release, payloads. They operate the arm with two control levers. One lever moves the arm up and down, and the other moves it from side to side. Another control allows the arm to grab or release the payload. Video cameras help astronauts see the payload and the arm. Astronauts must be careful when deploying and retrieving satellites. Most satellites fit snugly in the shuttle's payload bay. Tapping a satellite against one of the bay's walls could damage the satellite or the Shuttle.

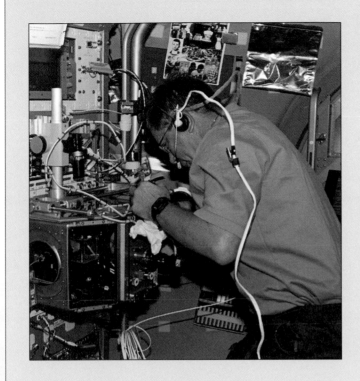

Experiments

On board the Shuttle, astronauts perform experiments in biology, electronics, metals, and chemistry. Scientists use the information the astronauts gather to learn about living in space. The unique conditions of weightlessness make many materials behave differently in space than on Earth. For example, some medicines are made with tiny crystals that grow perfectly in microgravity but not on Earth. Scientists believe that someday astronauts will be able to manufacture pure medications in space.

More hands, please

It takes much longer to finish a task on the Shuttle than it does on Earth. In microgravity, even changing flashlight batteries is complicated. The battery cover, used batteries, new batteries, and flashlight will float away if they are not secured. Astronauts often say that they wish they had more hands!

These astronauts are performing an experiment that tests a person's ability to react to objects in microgravity. This apparatus was designed by France's space agency, the **Centre National d'Études Spatiales**.

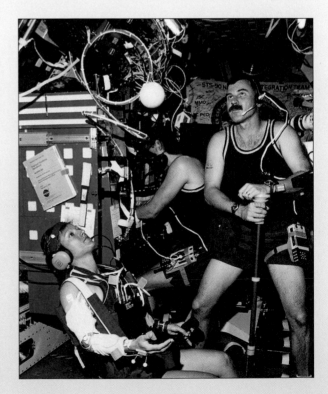

Space walking

Astronauts **space walk**, or move around outside the Shuttle, to perform jobs such as repairing satellites. They wear space suits, which allow them to breathe and control their body temperature outside the spacecraft. Astronauts use handholds and footholds to crawl around the outside of the Shuttle. Space suits weigh 300 pounds (136 kg) on Earth, but they weigh almost nothing in space!

*Astronauts wear **jetpacks** called **Manned Maneuvering Units**, or **MMUs**, to propel themselves from the Shuttle to a work site. They must watch the fuel gauge on the MMU, or they could be stranded in space!*

Overhead construction

Astronauts from many different countries are working together 250 miles (402 km) above Earth on the highest construction site in history! They are building the International Space Station, the first structure ever built in space. The station is so huge that it cannot be sent into space all at once. Separate **modules**, or pieces, are launched one at a time, and astronauts assemble them in space. A robotic arm is used to bring the pieces together. Astronauts then space walk to finish connecting the modules by screwing items into place and connecting wires.

Space tools

Astronauts use tools designed especially for use in space. For example, their hammers are filled with liquid to absorb impact. If the hammers were solid, the astronauts would get thrown backward every time they hit something. All the tools are **tethered**, or attached, to the astronaut's suit so they will not float away. It takes two separate actions to release the hook that holds a tool so it cannot come loose accidentally.

Eating and sleeping

The first astronauts had a limited choice of food—mashed food in metal tubes, freeze-dried powders, or bite-size chunks coated with gelatin. Space food has improved over the years. Today, astronauts choose from foods such as chicken à la king or shrimp cocktail. The meals are pre-cooked and pre-packaged. Some foods need only to be heated. Other food is dehydrated—the astronauts simply add water to it before eating.

Space dining

To eat their meal, astronauts attach food packages to a tray. The tray is strapped to their leg or attached to the wall with Velcro®. Most of the foods are sticky or saucy, so they can be eaten with forks and spoons. The food will not float away unless it is bumped or moved suddenly. Astronauts drink through straws that have a clamp. When they stop sucking, the clamp shuts the straw so that the liquid cannot escape.

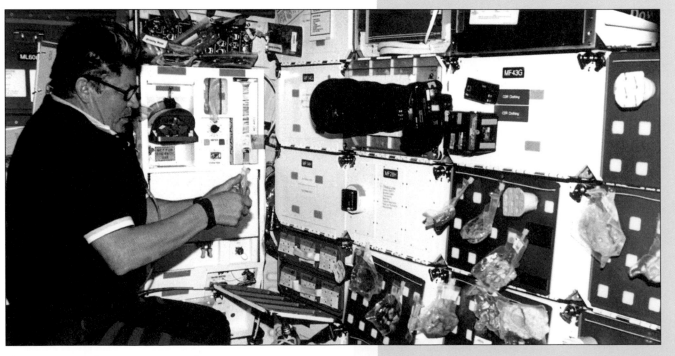

Astronauts take turns preparing meals for the crew.

Sleeping in space

In microgravity, astronauts sleep in their seats, in sleeping bags, in enclosed metal bunks, or even strapped to the walls! Since there is no "up" or "down" in microgravity, sleeping upright feels no different than sleeping horizontally. Astronauts do not need soft beds because their weightless bodies do not sink into a mattress.

Catching zzz's

The flight plan allows astronauts to sleep eight hours a day. Sometimes half the crew stays awake and works while the other half sleeps. If the whole crew sleeps at the same time, two people wear headsets to bed so they can hear alarms or receive messages from Mission Control.

Astronauts zip themselves into sleeping bags, which are attached to the wall with Velcro®.

Clean and healthy

In space, astronauts cannot shower or use a toilet as we do on Earth. Water does not flow down in microgravity—it floats in droplets. To clean themselves, astronauts soak a cloth, lather it with soap, and then wipe themselves clean. When they brush their teeth, astronauts cannot spit the toothpaste down the drain. The toothpaste would just float away! Instead, they spit into a tissue.

Astronauts wash their hair with a type of shampoo that does not need to be rinsed.

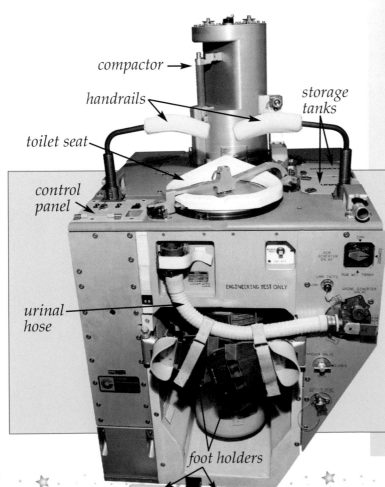

compactor →

handrails

storage tanks

toilet seat

control panel

urinal hose

foot holders

ENGINEERING TEST ONLY

The Shuttle's toilet
Space toilets use air instead of water to carry away waste. A hose acts like a vacuum to pull liquid waste away from an astronaut's body. Solid waste goes into a hole in the toilet. Air vents around the hole blow the waste into storage tanks. The toilet turns on and is ready to use when the seat is lifted.

Work that body

Microgravity is hard on an astronaut's body. It weakens bones, muscles, and organs such as the heart. Astronauts exercise every day to keep their body strong. They work out on machines such as the **ergometer**, shown left. The ergometer is like a stationary bicycle. The astronauts strap themselves to the machine so that they will not float away when exercising.

Free time

In space, astronauts do not have a lot of free time. When they do, they often spend it looking out the Shuttle's windows. Sometimes they play in microgravity—they turn somersaults in mid-air or play catch with small objects. Many astronauts listen to music before they fall asleep. NASA provides each crew member with a cassette player, and each astronaut can bring six tapes to play.

Astronauts can observe Earth through the Space Shuttle's top window.

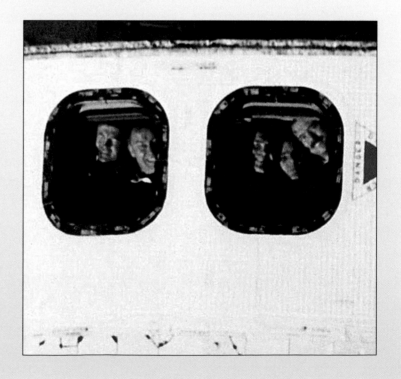

Coming home

The final stage of the mission is the process of reentry. As the Shuttle **deorbits**, it must hit Earth's **atmosphere** at the exact angle. Otherwise, it could bounce off into space or burn up as it moves through the air.

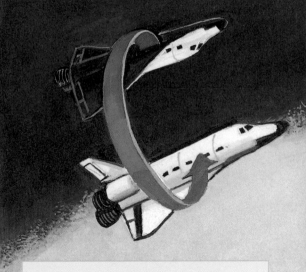

Getting used to gravity

The astronauts' brain and body are "confused" for awhile after they land. After being weightless for several days, their body feels too heavy to move on Earth. It is difficult for the astronauts to keep their balance. It takes up to an hour before the crew feels ready to stand and walk, and up to a week before they become fully used to the feel of gravity again.

1. The commander uses the maneuvering rockets to turn and lower the Shuttle toward the atmosphere. Once in the atmosphere, air creates **drag**, or resistance, which slows the Shuttle down. Computers now take over and guide the craft.

It's not over yet

After they land, the astronauts spend several days being tested by doctors. They also get **debriefed**, which means that scientists, supervisors, and other astronauts ask them questions about their mission. Debriefing provides NASA with important information that will be used when planning the next mission.

2. About 50 miles (80 km) above the ground, the atmosphere becomes thicker and creates more drag—the Shuttle slows down much faster. The astronauts' body feels very heavy. It is difficult for the astronauts to move or talk.

3. The **friction**, or rubbing, of the air against the Shuttle heats the air to thousands of degrees. A white-hot glow flares outside the Shuttle. The hot air blocks radio signals for a few minutes. The crew loses contact with Mission Control during this **radio blackout**.

4. As the Shuttle reaches the landing strip, the commander takes over the controls and has only one chance to land. The Shuttle has no fuel to carry it up for a second try.

A year on orbit

The average Space Shuttle mission lasts one to two weeks. Can you imagine spending six months in space? That is what cosmonauts and astronauts from around the world do at Russia's *Mir* space station. *Mir* has been orbiting Earth for nearly fifteen years. It soon will be replaced by the International Space Station.

Activities such as cleaning are very important on *Mir*. The astronauts must clean the entire station every weekend to keep it free of germs. They also exercise every day to keep their body healthy in microgravity. Unmanned spacecraft dock with *Mir* every few months to bring supplies such as food and oxygen.

Why a space station?

A space station offers great opportunities to scientists. Microgravity research provides unique information to help cure diseases. Unlike on the Shuttle, experiments in space can be conducted for months at a time because *Mir* does not need to return to Earth.

An electrical fire once broke out on the Mir *space station. The astronauts on board could not jump out of a window as they would on Earth. Fortunately, the astronauts extinguished the fire quickly, and no one was hurt.*

Risky business

Astronauts put their lives in the hands of thousands of other people. They rely on engineers and mechanics to provide them with a safe spacecraft. Technicians carefully prepare and inspect every part of the spacecraft before its launch. If something goes wrong in space, the astronauts have no way to escape.

Lost in space

Space is full of tiny particles of dust called **micrometeors**. This debris flies through space at thousands of miles per hour. At this speed, even small pieces could kill an astronaut on impact! Space suits are made of a strong material that protects space walkers from micrometeors.

Deadly accidents

Astronauts have a dangerous job, but there have been only three deadly accidents in history. In 1967, three astronauts scheduled to fly the first Apollo mission were killed when a fire consumed the capsule on the launch pad. In 1971, three cosmonauts died when their craft lost its air pressure. The only major accident on a Space Shuttle occurred in 1986, when the Space Shuttle Challenger exploded shortly after leaving the ground. The fuel tank explosion killed all seven crew members.

After the Challenger disaster, NASA did not launch any Shuttles for two years. This time was spent perfecting equipment to prevent further accidents.

Future astronauts

Do you dream of becoming an astronaut? Even if you are too young to become an astronaut candidate, you can go to **SPACE CAMP**®. The first Space Camp started in Huntsville, Alabama in 1982. Now there are Space Camps in California and Florida, as well as other countries such as Canada and Japan. At these camps, kids learn about astronauts and train on equipment that prepares them for life in space!

Becoming a candidate

To be considered for astronaut training, you must meet a list of qualifications. You should be in good physical shape and between 4'10" and 6'4" inches (1.45 to 1.93 m) tall. It is also important to earn a university degree in math, science, or engineering. To learn more about becoming an astronaut, write to NASA and ask for an application package. Send your letter to:

Astronaut Selection Office
Mail Code AHX
Johnson Space Center
Houston, Texas 77058-3696

*The **Zero-G wall** allows campers to feel the sensation of microgravity. They sit in chairs attached to a system of wires and springs.*

Stimulating simulators!

Space Camp uses all kinds of simulators to help train the campers. Some were used during the Mercury and Gemini projects. The Shuttle simulators, however, are similar to those used by real astronauts today. Campers are split into teams. They train to be pilots and mission specialists. Campers "fly" simulated missions in which they work as a team on the Shuttle simulator. Children learn about the procedures in Mission Control and help their fellow campers during their mission.

*(above) A system of springs attached to the **microgravity training chair** allows campers to feel what it is like to walk on the Moon!*

(left) Campers at the Mission Control mock-up use headsets to communicate with people in the Space Shuttle mock-up. Together, they carry out missions.

Glossary

astronomy The study of outer space

atmosphere The gases that surround a planet

centrifuge A machine in which people experience the pressure felt during the liftoff of a spacecraft

egress An emergency exit from a spacecraft before it reaches space

ergometer A machine on a spacecraft that astronauts use to exercise

free fall The fall of an object through the atmosphere without any resistance, such as a parachute, to slow the object

gravity The force that pulls things toward the center of a star, planet, or moon

mass The measure of the amount of matter an object contains

microgravity Very little gravity; weightlessness

micrometeor A tiny dust particle found in space

mission specialist An astronaut who is responsible for Shuttle systems, crew activity planning, meals, and payload bay activity

module A section of a space station

navigation The practice of planning a course for a vehicle such as an aircraft or spacecraft

orbit (n) The path taken by a craft around a planet or moon; (v) To travel around a planet or moon

payload specialist A person other than an astronaut who works in the Shuttle's laboratory

physics The study of energy and matter

pressure suit An air-tight suit astronauts wear to survive conditions in space; a space suit

satellite An object that travels in a particular orbit around a body in space

simulator A machine that helps astronauts train by reproducing experiences in space

Index

1 2 3 4 5 6 7 8 9 0 Printed in the U.S.A. 9 8 7 6 5 4 3 2 1 0

DATE DUE

JAN 2 8				
SEP 1 3				
Pflug '03				
SEP 5 -				
Bordell 1/04				
APR 2 3				
OCT 3 0				

J. C. BUSH SCHOOL